Version 2.0

Version 2.0

More BYTE-ing Humor from
The 5th Wave by Rich Tennant

Andrews and McMeel
A Universal Press Syndicate Company
Kansas City

ISBN: 0-8362-1783-7

Library of Congress Catalog Card Number: 94-73238

There are a lot of funny things
about the computer industry.
But not many.

—Paraphrased Goldwynism

"Excuse me — is anyone here NOT talking about multimedia computing?"

7

"It's the break we've been waiting for, Lieutenant.
The thieves figured out how to turn on one of the stolen
video conferencing monitors."

At a football game, the Real Programmer is the one
comparing the plays against his simulation printout.

"We sort of have our own way of predicting network problems."

That morning, Frank and Mona Tubman tried running
multiple applications through Windows on an OS/2
platform with their 286 DinQue PC. The hard disk,
seeking power from whatever source, began tapping
appliances throughout the household electrical system,
eventually sucking time itself from the wall clocks,
thrusting the couple into an irreversible time-loop!

"I'm sorry, but Mr. Halloran is being chased by six midgets with poison boomerangs through a maze in the dungeon of a castle. If he finds his way out and gets past the minotaur, he'll call you right back; otherwise try again Thursday."

13

15

Bob's decision not to be connected to the computer network caused some suspicion on the part of those who were.

"Compatibility? No problem. This baby comes in over a dozen designer colors."

"Yes, I think it's an error message."

"I suppose this all has something to do with
the new math."

18

22

"Oops, I forgot to log off again."

"You know, if we can all keep the tittering down, I, for one, would like to hear more about Ken's new pointing device for notebooks."

INDUSTRY WATCHERS PREDICTED THAT IN THE NEAR FUTURE, MONDOTECH CORP. WILL UP THE ANTE IN THE **AT** CLONE MARKET BY INTRODUCING A PC THAT'S COMPATIBLE WITH BOTH IBM, APPLE, AND KIRBY VACUUM CLEANERS.

"Well this has sure turned out to be a
Mickey Mouse system."

"It says, 'Seth – Please see us about your idea to wrap newsletter text around company logo. Production.'"

"OK, technically this should work. Judy, type the word, 'Goodyear' all caps, bold face, at 700 point type size."

28

"Yes, we still have a few bugs in the word processing software.
By the way, here's a memo from marketing."

"The funny thing is, I never knew they HAD desktop publishing software for paper shredders."

"Whoa, hold the phone! It says, 'The electricity coming out of a surge protector is generally cleaner and safer than that going into one, unless-UN-LESSS– you are standing in a bucket of water.'"

WHY DOGS DON'T USE LAPTOPS

"Miss Lamont, I'm filing the congregation database under 'SOULS,' my sermons under 'GRACE,' and the financial contribution spreadsheet under 'AMEN.'"

"Well, I never thought I'd see the day I could say I dialed in a modem via a stat mux into a dedicated port on a communications processor...by accident."

Advances in the area of pen-based recognition systems are hampered by the preponderance of pencil chewing among researchers.

"Hey, Dad, is it all right if I window your computer?"

"For futher thoughts on that subject, I'm going to download Leviticus and go through the menu to Job, chapter 2, verse 6, file 'J'. It reads ..."

"This Corel color scheme is REALLY going to give our presentation STYLE!"

35

"Hey, Dad — guess how many Milk Duds
fit inside your disk drive."

"You know that guy who bought all that software?
His check has a warranty that says it's tendered as is
and has no fitness for any particular purpose including,
but not limited to, cashing."

"That's right, Daddy will double your salary if you make him more OS/2 applications."

"It's an integrated software package designed to help unclutter your life."

39

Artists' signature PCs

"I'll be with you as soon as I execute a few more commands."

41

"They're really trying to make this a 'something for everyone' convention this year."

"He said, 'Why buy just a word processor when you can get one with a math and graphics link capable of doing schematics of an F100 aircraft engine?' And I thought, well, we never buy Toastems without bran ..."

"And to complete our multimedia presentation ... "

Real Programmers either smoke two packs of cigarettes a day, or they don't smoke at all.

"It's a memo from software documentation.
It's either an explanation of how the new satellite
communications network functions, or directions for
replacing batteries in the smoke detectors."

"My gosh, Barbara, if you don't think it's worth going a
couple of weeks without dinner so we can afford an
optical drive file server, just say so."

"Now, when someone rings my doorbell, the current goes to a scanner that digitizes the audio impulses and sends the image to the PC where it's converted to a Pict file. The image is then animated, compressed, and sent via high-speed modem to an automated phone service that sends an e-mail message back to tell me someone was at my door 40 minutes ago."

"Shoot, that's nothing! Watch me spin him!"

"You know, I liked you a whole lot more on the Internet."

"Now, just when the heck did I integrate THAT into the system?"

"I just moved into one of those Smart-Houses that you can phone up and have it do things. Well, the other day I got a wrong number, and before I could hang up, the guy turned the lights off, fed the dog, and drained the Jacuzzi."

"… And, hey—what about the names of some of these companies—Peachtree, Apple. What are we supposed to do, program these things or peel 'em? I don't know if these things go on a desk or in a bowl."

"His name is D'Marco D'Magician. He's helping us tap into some unregulated wavelengths for our cellular PDAs."

53

"I just bought a new computer that comes with tons of additional memory, in fact, for an extra one hundred dollars it'll even carry a grudge."

"So this guy says he needs to get rid of his Apple PC because it's getting too old, and the other guy says 'How old is it?' And the first guy says, 'This Apple's so old, it's starting to attract fruit flies!' AAAAAHH HAHAHAHAHAHA thank you thank you!"

"... And you're claiming that the source code used for the Microsoft Corp. GUI was actually authored by you as the Gumby user interface?!"

56

57

"Hurry, Stuart!! Hurry!! The screen's starting to flicker out!!"

"My God, you've done it! Millions of microscopic Slinky toys moving across circuits at the speed of light forming the first SLINKY OPERATING SYSTEM!"

Kent couldn't understand what all the fuss about Pen-Based computing was — he'd been using it for years.

61

"Quick kids! Your mother's flaming someone
on the Internet!"

"We should have this fixed in Version 2.0."

"It was between that and new classroom computers."

"... And the winner of the Vaporware Award will receive this six foot gold statuette and this check in the amount of one hundred billion dollars."

Real Programmers HATE decaffeinated coffee.

"Yo—I think we've got a new kind of virus here!"

"He must be a Macintosh user — there's a wristwatch icon etched on his retina."

The 500 Channel multimedia future

69

"For us, it was total integration or nothing.
For instance — at this terminal alone I can get
departmental data, printer and storage resources, ESPN,
Home Shopping Network, AND the Movie Channel."

"I'm always amazed at the technological advances
made at ad agencies and PR firms."

"Well, heck — I can't step away from the computer for a second
without you birds gettin' all ruffled about it."

5th Wave Power Tip: To increase application speed, punch the Command Key over and over and over as rapidly as possible. The computer will sense your impatience and move your data along more quickly than if you just sat and waited. Hint: This also works on elevator buttons and crosswalk signals.

73

While upgrading to Windows 3.1, Tonto, the scout, embarrasses himself by taking the wrong path reference back to the directory.

"You'd better get out here—one of the links in the network is acting up."

After spending hours trying to get the system up and running, Carl discovers that everything had been plugged into a "Clapper" light socket when he tries to kill a mosquito.

"It's Kevin from 'PC Fix–It,' only they're trying to change their image so I'm supposed to say it's 'Menlo Park Jones' from 'Raiders of the DOS Arc.'"

IT'S REALLY QUITE SIMPLE. WITH THE REVISED MAINFRAME PRICING POLICY, YOU'LL BE CHARGED ONE-QUARTER OF THE PREVIOUS PRICE PER CPU BASED ON A 3-TIERED SITE LICENSING AGREEMENT FOR UP TO 12 USERS, AFTER WHICH A 5-TIERED SYSTEM IS EMPLOYED FOR UP TO 64 USERS WITHIN THE ORIGINAL 4-TIERED SYSTEM FOR NEW CUSTOMERS USING OLD SOFTWARE OR OLD CUSTOMERS USING NEW SOFTWARE ON EACH OF THREE CPUS RUNNING A NEW OLD OPERATING SYSTEMS SITE LICENSED UNDER THE OLD NEW AGREEMENT BUT ONLY ON THURSDAYS WITH LESS THAN 10 PEOPLE IN THE ROOM, ...

"We've expanded the memory on this one so many times it's starting to get stretch marks."

See zany programmers turn Hi-Tech into Hi-Jinks as they kluge 'till they lose in a belt-busting spaghetti code feast of nutty networks, silly software, and hardy-har-hardware.

WHERE **NOT** TO USE A TOUCH-SCREEN COMPUTER

81

"What concerns me about the Information Superhighway is that it appears to be entering though Brent's bedroom."

"Why a 4GL toaster? I don't think you'd ask that question if you thought a minute about how to balance the maximization of toast development productivity against toaster resource utilization in a multi-diner environment."

Re·al Pro·gram·mers

Real Programmers don't sleep — their systems just temporarily go down.

"How's that for fast scrolling?"

"We hardly get any complaints from users anymore. Think it's because we hired a troglodyte to run the department?"

"I don't know —some parts of the network seem just fine and other parts seem to be completely out of control."

"It happened around the time we subscribed to an on-line service."

88

"The system came bundled with a graphics board, a spreadsheet, and the developer's out-of-work nephew."

"You've plugged your mouse into the electric shaver outlet again."

93

"I think 'Fuzzy Logic' is an important technology too. I'm just not sure we should feature it as part of our tax preparation software."

95

As fate would have it, the release of Wayne's wallet computer would be postponed for several weeks.

"WELL, I'm really looking forward to seeing this wireless data transmission system of yours, Mudnick."

"Oh sure, it'll float all right, but integration's
gonna be a killer."

Shriners network

"Well'p — there goes the ambiance."

PROVING THAT BIGGER ISN'T ALWAYS BEST, A CONTRACT TO BUILD A COMPUTERIZED SONAR TRACKING SYSTEM FOR THE U.S. NAVY IS AWARDED TO TROOP 708 OF THE BAYONNE, NEW JERSEY EAGLE SCOUTS.

"We never had much luck building a decent handwriting recognition system, but Roy there's done real good making a flat screen notebook that reads lips."

"And finally, do you feel your client/server environment
keeps you well connected to your department?"

"No, that's not a pie chart. It's just a corn chip
that got scanned into the document."

103